THREE OCCULT FEMALE SPIRITS

JEZEBEL

DELILAH   ATHALIAH

Ethel A. Scott

Copyright © 2011 by Ethel A Scott

Three Occult Female Spirits
by Ethel A Scott

Printed in the United States of America

ISBN 9781613793671

All rights reserved solely by the author. The author guarantees all contents are original and do not infringe upon the legal rights of any other person or work. No part of this book may be reproduced in any form without the permission of the author. The views expressed in this book are not necessarily those of the publisher.

Unless otherwise indicated, Bible quotations are taken from The King James Study Bible. Copyright © 1988 by Liberty University, Thomas Nelson Publishers.

www.xulonpress.com

Dedication

I dedicate this book to the only wise God, our Savior, be glory and majesty, dominion and power, both now and forever, as the Father unveiled to me the satanic strategies of the unseen world.

I especially give thanks to my husband Willard Scott, my sister Bridget Vereen, my daughters Takela and Tashena Alexander, my grandsons Dontrell, Aaron, Calab and Ahmad. I'd also like to thank Christina Fields and Melonese Grant for their timely assistance in support as well as prayers. Finally, I dedicate this book to my beloved sister Wanda Williams (who resides with the Lord).

> "For I neither received it of man, neither was I taught it, but by the revelation of Jesus Christ".
>
> **Galatians 1:12**

Youtube: Apostle Scott Ministries
Facebook: Apostle Scott
Email: Toldministries@msn.com
Mailing Address: P. O. Box 470152
                   Miami, FL 33247

Forward

The 20th Century has known some women who where very deadly and also very dangerous. Ruthless women like Bonnie Parker, Kate Barker and Ailen Wuornois. Each of these women were notorious and infamous for either killing people or consenting to people being killed. Sometimes it is hard for us as people to see women as anything but beautiful and sweet (after all women are known as the weaker vessel). Women have also been known as the better half and the fairer sex.

Often times when I think of women I think of sweet kind and loving, but I need to keep in mind that nothing except God is completely good and pure and righteous, so with women as well as every thing else there are exceptions. The bible states in the book of Ecclesiastes 1:9, "The thing that hath been, it is that which shall be; and that which is done is that which shall be done: and there is no new thing under the sun", and with that in mind long before there was a Bonnie Parker or a Kate Barker or even an Aileen Wuornos they had predecessors in ancient times. Women like Delilah, Jezebel and Athaliah are the forerunners of the three 20th Century women that I mentioned earlier. Just like Aileen Wuornos was a seducer of men so was Delilah just like Aileen wuornos, Bonnie Parker and Kate or Ma Barker killed men so did Jezebel and Athaliah. Jezebel enjoyed controlling men and her daughter Athaliah enjoyed controlling her son as did Ma Barker, who controlled her four sons.

We could examine the similarities between the two sets of women even more extensively but let me save some of the information in the book for the book. This book was written to unmask and unveil an assignment that has been set against mankind for its destruction. This assignment was given to one of the most unlikely sources, some women who are not even aware of the assignment that they are operating in. Through revelations, given of God, Apostle Scott leads us on an incredible journey as the tricks of Satan are unlocked. Because the bible says, "My people are destroyed for a lack of knowledge" Apostle Scott has written this book for all to be informed, so may the Lord add a blessing to those who are readers of this book and let it also be edifying to them.

- Willard Scott

Endorsements

I thank God for the Massa anointing upon Apostle Scott's life that has lead her to publish a book about the "Three Occult Female Spirits". This book will give men and women a better understanding about the three occult female spirits, Delilah, Jezebel and Athaliah. My prayer is that the apostolic sons & daughters will unlock the hidden mysteries of God written in this book to advance the kingdom of God for generations and generations to come. Apostle Scott, I love you and may God continue to bless you in your endeavors.

- Janice Wright

Apostle Scott is truly an apostolic voice, one whom God has sent forth in this time for apostolic reformation in the church of today. She has given to the body of Christ the teachings, impartations and principles in the order of apostolic dimensions with demonstration and power. The anointing of revelation upon her life brings spirituality truth to the church at large with this mission in her heart. We pray the church will embrace this apostolic move that God has placed upon her life that will develop us in fulfilling the charge of Christ in apostolic dimension.

- Apostle Gaskin

I personally welcome all of you to Apostle Ethel Scott's new book release title "Three Occult Female Spirits". In this exciting book you will discover the who, what, when and how people turn to unnatural sexual gratification and satisfaction. The Holy Spirit has allowed her to tap into the spirit world to reveal to the people of today why the sons and daughters are trapped into their unnatural behavior. In this life changing book she has exposed the enemy and his works so that the people can be set free and no longer be held in bondage. I decree and declare that this book shall be read by millions of people and it shall be number one on the New York Times Best Sellers list.

- Martha M Gathers

The book, the Three Occult Female Spirits is a must read. If you have experienced extreme resistance against building your ministry on dimensional levels, this book is a must have. This book may help you to recognize which particular spirit you are in opposition with, how to warfare against these particular territorial spirits and how to come out of the

battle victoriously. Apostle E. Scott, thank you for another dimension of knowledge that will bring more victories in the lives of people who read this book.
- Kanitha Wooten

I decree & declare that the apostolic and prophetic intercessors will make intercession on behalf of your servant Apostle E. Scott, as these prophetic writings go out to the four corners of the earth to break barriers, break tradition and set your people free from the hand of the enemy. I decree revelation knowledge to be their portion as they begin to read the word that's coming forth now. I also decree that the sons and daughters lives be elevated through the word of God in the name of Jesus.
- Celetha Riley

This book (Three Occult Female Spirits) is a warfare tool against the three female spirits that are so prevalent in the world today. We often hear the world's definition of what Delilah, Jezebel and Althaliah are suppose to be. This book will show us just how far we are from the real manifestations of these spirits and also teach us how to break their powers. I have sat under the tutelage of Apostle E. Scott for ten years and I have seen the evidence of these prayers and how God has given her the mysteries to be a vessel to help destroy the enemies power and control over his people. I know that whoever embraces this tool and any other book that she has written, will be able to tear the kingdom of Satan DOWN!

- Elishea Moore

It is such an honor to speak on behalf of this author, Apostle E. Scott, whom I've had the pleasure of knowing for 16 years. The knowledge and insight that the Lord has entrusted her with on spiritual warfare is phenomenal. This book is the answer to render these three occult female spirits, that are harboring over God's people, ineffective as well as null and void. These spirits have operated in high places due to a lack of knowledge concerning their influences, cunningness and schemes. To the one that possesses this book, they will obtain great knowledge and it will be a great blessing in their lives as well as many others lives. The false kingdoms that have been set up by these triple threat women are just like the walls of Jericho and they are coming down!

- Melonese Grant

First, I would like to thank our Lord and Savior Jesus Christ for giving Apostle E. Scott such wisdom and divine revelation to the secret mysteries of God. I truly bless God for placing me within a ministry where the spiritual leader is always in tune with God's voice and she is not afraid of preaching the truth in season and out of season. Apostle E. Scott is not afraid of sharing any spiritual insight that she has received from God with the Apostolic sons & daughters in the community, territories, regions, and or nations. My prayer is that those who read this book about the "Three Occult Female Spirits" will have a desire to be freed from any one of these demonic spirits that have possessed or oppressed them. In reading this book, I'm reminded of the woman with the issue of blood, she had such a desire to be healed that she would not allow anything or anyone to stop her deliverance. Sometimes, we have to push beyond where we are and not be ashamed of our issues but have a desire for a breakthrough in order to be healed. Today, receive your breakthrough, be healed and be the woman or man of God that God created you to be from the beginning of time. After all, you were created in His image!

- Christina Fields

TABLE OF CONTENTS

Chapter 1:
  Demonology 17
  The Reality of Demons 31
  Demons Seek Embodiment 34

Chapter 2:
  The Three Dimension of Man 37
  Demonic Attacks Commissioned to Man's
  Spirit 43

Chapter 3:
  The Unveiling 55
  The Three Female Spirits 60

Chapter 4:
  The Spirit of Delilah 64

Chapter 5:
  The Spirit of Jezebel 81

Chapter 6:
  The Spirit of Athaliah 104

Chapter 1

DEMONOLOGY

I. Definitions and Concepts

Demonic Possession - The control of a victim's personality and behavior by evil demonic spirits.

Matthew 12:22   Then was brought unto him one possessed with a devil, blind, and dumb: and he healed him, insomuch that the blind and dumb both spake and saw.

Luke 4: 31 – 36   And came down to Capernaum, a city of Galilee, and taught them on the sabbath days. And they were astonished at his doctrine: for his word was with power. And in the synagogue there was a man, which had a spirit of an unclean devil, and cried out with a loud voice, Saying, Let us alone; what have we to do with thee, thou Jesus of Nazareth? art thou come to destroy us? I know thee who thou art; the Holy One of God. And Jesus rebuked him, saying, Hold thy peace, and come out of him. And when the devil had thrown him in the midst, he came out of him, and hurt him not. And they were all amazed, and spake among themselves, saying, What a word is this! for with authority and power he commandeth the unclean spirits, and they come out.

Demonic Affliction - Demons that are able to afflict physical infirmities.

Matthew 17:15 – 18   Lord, have mercy on my son: for he is lunatick, and sore vexed: for ofttimes he falleth into the fire, and oft into the water. And I brought him to thy disciples, and they could not cure him. Then Jesus answered and said, O faithless and perverse generation, how long shall I be with you? how long shall I suffer you?

"seizures"

Three Occult Female Spirits

bring him hither to me. And Jesus rebuked the devil; and he departed out of him: and the child was cured from that very hour.

Demonic Oppression - Demonic activity that can burden one physically, spiritually and mentally.

Principalities - The lowest class of demons, of the systematic order of Ephesians 6:12. They demonstrate the manifestation of the ruling demons.

Powers - The second level of demons that equips, empowers and gives authority to the lower rank demons.

Rulers - Are ruling demons that Govern and control actions and behaviors. This demon is known as the strongman.

Spiritual Wickedness in high places - This is Satan himself, he is known as

Three Occult Female Spirits

	the prince of the power of the air.
Ephesians 2:2 -	Wherein in time past ye walked according to the course of this world, according to the prince of the power of the air, the spirit that now worketh in the children of disobedience:
Spirit of Delilah -	A demonic seducing spirit that is able to operate in either male or female.
Spirit of Jezebel -	A bi-gender demonic dominating spirit.
Spirit of Athaliah -	A bi-gender demonic spirit that kills the male seeds.
Spirit of Nabor -	A churlish man, that makes bad decisions or judgments and his wife must intercede for him.

1 Samuel 25:2-3, 9-11, 14-19, 23-25a
And there was a man in Maon, whose possessions were in Carmel; and the man was very great, and he had three thousand sheep, and a thousand

goats: and he was shearing his sheep in Carmel. Now the name of the man was Nabal; and the name of his wife Abigail: and she was a woman of good understanding, and of a beautiful countenance: but the man was churlish and evil in his doings; and he was of the house of Caleb. And when David's young men came, they spake to Nabal according to all those words in the name of David, and ceased. And Nabal answered David's servants, and said, Who is David? and who is the son of Jesse? there be many servants now days that break away every man from his master. Shall I then take my bread, and my water, and my flesh that I have killed for my shearers, and give it unto men, whom I know not whence they be? But one of the young men told Abigail, Nabal's wife, saying, Behold, David sent messengers out of the wilderness to salute our master; and he railed on them. But the men were very good unto us, and we were not hurt, neither missed we any thing, as long as we were conversant with them, when we were in the fields: They were a wall unto us both by night and day, all the while we were with them keeping the sheep. Now therefore know and consider what thou wilt do; for evil is determined against our master, and against all his household: for he is such a son of Belial, that a man cannot speak to him. Then Abigail made haste, and took two hundred loaves, and two bottles of wine, and five sheep ready dressed, and five measures of parched corn, and an hundred clusters of raisins, and two hundred cakes of figs, and laid them on asses. And she said unto her servants, Go on before me; behold, I come after you. But she told not her husband Nabal. And when Abigail saw David, she hasted, and lighted off the ass, and fell before David on her face, and bowed herself to the ground, And fell at his feet, and said, Upon me, my lord, upon me let this iniquity be: and let thine handmaid, I pray thee, speak in thine audience, and hear the words of thine handmaid. Let not my lord, I pray thee, regard this man of

Belial, even Nabal: for as his name is, so is he;

Spirit of Saul - A spiritual leader that lives in only partial obedience to God.

Spirit of Samson - An anointed man of God that wants instant sexual gratification.

Judges 14:3 Then his father and his mother said unto him, Is there never a woman among the daughters of thy brethren, or among all my people, that thou goest to take a wife of the uncircumcised Philistines? And Samson said unto his father, Get her for me; for she pleaseth me well.

Effeminate - A man that is marked by weakness. A man that is soft, delicate and extremely gentle to an unmanly degree in traits and behavior. He functions best in a life of ease.

(*Reference: Dictionary.com - Effeminate means an offensive term used to describe a man whose behavior, appearance, or speech is considered to be similar to that traditionally associated with women or girls.)

Spirit of Ahab - A man that is dominated and governed by his wife.

Spirit of Tamar - A female who has experienced incestuous sexual abuse.

2 Samuel 13:14 Howbeit he would not hearken unto her voice: but, being stronger than she, forced her, and lay with her.

Spirit of Amnon - A brother who commits incest with his sister.

2 Samuel 13:11 – 12 And when she had brought them unto him to eat, he took hold of her, and said unto her, Come lie with me, my sister. And she answered him, Nay, my brother, do not force me; for no such thing ought to be done in Israel: do not thou this folly.

Three Occult Female Spirits

Spirit of Reuben -   A son who commits incest with his father's wife.

    Genesis 35:22   And it came to pass, when Israel dwelt in that land, that Reuben went and lay with Bilhah his father's concubine: and Israel heard it. Now the sons of Jacob were twelve:

Spirit of Gomer -   A female spirit of harlotry, an adulterous wife.

    Hosea 1:2   The beginning of the word of the LORD by Hosea. And the LORD said to Hosea, Go, take unto thee a wife of whoredoms and children of whoredoms: for the land hath committed great whoredom, departing from the LORD.

Spirit of Rehoboam -   A man or leader that refuses godly counsel and wisdom. This spirit will lead them near destruction.

Succubus -   A female sexual demon that seeks intercourse with males. This spirit

	targets his body, soul, and Id.
Incubus -	A male sexual demon that seeks sexual intercourse with females. This spirit targets her body, soul, and Id.
Spirit of Korah -	A demonic spirit in ministry that promotes rebellion against spiritual authority.
Spirit of Adam -	A Godly man that heeds ungodly council from his wife.
Spirit of Judas -	A person that promotes betrayal.
Spirit of Absalom -	A person that betrays his own kinsmen, and rises up against his own family, and forms an alliance with others to destroy his own spiritual authority figure.

Three Occult Female Spirits

Spirit of Michal - A wife who despises her husband's anointing and his relationship with God.

    2 Samuel 6:16 And as the ark of the LORD came into the city of David, Michal Saul's daughter looked through a window, and saw king David leaping and dancing before the LORD; and she despised him in her heart.

Spirit of Manasseh - A controlling male spirit of authority, that has no respect for righteousness. Deals in witchcraft, Satanism, child sacrifice and significant others. This spirit can be found in child pornographers who sacrifice and traumatize children's three-fold nature (body, spirit, and soul) through pornography.

Spirit of Cain - A brother that murders his brother.

    Genesis 4:8 And Cain talked with Abel his brother: and it came to pass, when they were in the field, that Cain rose up against Abel his brother, and slew him.

ID - The id is the pleasure seeking aspect of the personality. It desires instant bodily gratification.

Ego - The ego is the reality component of the personality. It controls our desires and normally expresses them in appropriate ways.

Superego - Within the superego, there are two components; the conscience and the ego-ideal. The conscience is where we have the ability to feel and understand. It contains our prohibition and our restrictions, preventing man's conscience from doing certain things. The ego-ideal contains man's aspirations and values that he or she strives for.

Spiritual Warfare - When Christians are engaging and battling in the unseen and the spiritual realm against the demonic forces of darkness.

Binding & Loosing - Matt. 16:18 - 19, And I say also unto thee, That thou art Peter, and upon this rock I will build my church; and the gates of hell shall not prevail against it. And I will give unto thee the keys of the kingdom of heaven: and whatsoever thou shalt bind on earth shall be bound in heaven: and whatsoever thou shalt loose on earth shall be loosed in heaven.

Prophetic Intercession or Praying - Is the act of proclaiming, declaring and decreeing the word and the mind of God.

Spiritual Cleansing - Refer to my book "Prayers for Spiritual Warfare".

Seducing Spirit - Preys upon a victim, taking him or her into captivity and then this spirit turns his victim over to another spirit. This spirit emulates John the Baptist, because John was a forerunner for Jesus Christ. The seducing spirit is a forerunner, and prepares the way for other demonic spirits. An example of this is, the seducing spirit is a forerunner for perversion, lying, divination, and the Delilah spirit.

Prince of Persia - A national fallen demon that governs regions, operates under Satan as a god of this world. He delay prayers, divine revelation and opposes truth. When dealing with Prince of Persia there is much angelic warfarring.

II. The Reality of Demons

Demonology is the study of demons. Demons are evil spiritual beings that are at war with God and humanity. They are fallen angles who joined the kingdom of Satan in rebellion against God. Some of the fallens were rebellious angels assigned to mankind as the watchers.

Isaiah 14:12	How art thou fallen from heaven, O Lucifer, son of the morning! how art thou cut down to the ground, which didst weaken the nations!
Revelation 12:9	And the great dragon was cast out, that old serpent, called the devil, and Satan, which deceiveth the whole world: he was cast out into the earth, and his angels were cast out with him.
Genesis 6:4	There were giants in the earth in those days; and also after that, when the sons of God came in unto the daughters of men, and they bare children to them, the same became mighty men which were of old, men of renown.

Jude 1:6	And the angels which kept not their first estate, but left their own habitation, he hath reserved in everlasting chains under darkness unto the judgment of the great day.

Satan has a systematic plan to disqualify man, destroy his purpose and also his identity. The devil and his demons are real and they possess personalities.

- They demonstrate <u>intelligence</u>.

Mark 3:11	And unclean spirits, when they saw him, fell down before him, and cried, saying, Thou art the Son of God.

- They exhibit <u>emotions</u>.

Matthew 8:31	So the devils besought him, saying, If thou cast us out, suffer us to go away into the herd of swine.

- They exhibit <u>desires</u>.

Luke 22:31	And the Lord said, Simon, Simon, behold, Satan hath desired to have you, that he may sift you as wheat:

Three Occult Female Spirits

The devil has a systematic seductive plan to destroy mankind and bring men into captivity through three female demonic spirits. They are the spirit of Delilah, the spirit of Jezebel, and the spirit of Athaliah. His plan is that mankind does not come into the knowledge of his demonic and seductive strategy, via the form of a woman. Man's greatest weakness is women and there are some women who are demonized to keep the male seed in bondage. Some women are oppressed and possessed by these spirits that desire to be free.

Satan's desire is to hold the man into captivity and prevent the male seed from recovering from this demonic attack. Satan will also commission these female spirits to oppress and possess the male and female gender.

| 2 Timothy 2:26 | And that they may recover themselves out of the snare of the devil, who are taken captive by him at his will. |

Demons are real; they can possess, oppress, afflict, pervert, and promote idolatry. They can promote anything that opposes the plan of God.

III. Demons Seeks Embodiment

Demons cannot effectively carry out the plan of Satan, unless they possess or oppress a physical body.

- **Demonic attack to the soulish realm** (Read: Mark 5:1 – 20)

    - A legion of demons possessed a man. They held this man in captivity at a graveyard and attacked his soulish realm. This man was depressed, suicidal and emotionally disturbed. There are men that are bound in a dead place and it appears that they cannot come alive in any aspects of their life. Many of these men are oppressed and depressed to the point of suicide. There are many young men, that are angry, emotionally disturbed and they have a desire to kill. In the book of Mark, this man has the same characteristics of many men today that are possessed by demons.

- **Demonic attack to the body** (Read: Mark 3:1 – 5)

    o A demon possessed a man's hand and caused it to be crippled. I believe this man was not able to function as he desired. Jesus cast the demon out and the man was made whole. Today, there are men whose lives are crippled and they have experienced demonic attacks preventing them from living productive lives, from accomplishing their visions, and becoming effective in achieving their goals and aspirations. These men exist only and feel utterly incomplete.

- **Demonic attach to the spirit** (Read: Luke 4:31 – 36)

    o A demon that knew who Jesus was, possessed a man's life and the man did not want to have anything to do with Jesus. He wanted to be left alone. In these days, there are men, who know who Jesus is, but they have demonic spirits that have oppressed or possessed them. They refuse to covenant with God and they refuse to establish a relationship with Jesus. These men just want to be left alone to live an apathetic life style. One illustration of this is (Mr. Couch Potato) who's life is his work, the television and the sofa. Another illustration is (Mr. Hobbyist) who's into himself and the things that interest him. Finally there is (Mr. Phobia) who is dominated by many fears and insecurities. He desires to be left alone to conceal his true condition.

Chapter 2

THE THREE DIMENSION OF MAN

I. Man's Creation

Genesis 1:26a - And God said, Let us make man in our image, after our likeness.

God is a spirit, and does not possess flesh and bones. In this verse God is speaking to the other two persons of the trinity, God the Son and God the Holy Ghost. God deals in numbers. The number three represents the Godhead; The Father, Son, and the Holy Spirit. The number three also represents:

    A. The Three Steps in the Creation of Man:
        (1). God's Spirit - Genesis 1:26 - And God said, Let us make man in our

image, after our likeness. God gives man a spirit.

(2). <u>The dust of the ground</u> - Genesis 2:7a - And the Lord God formed man of the dust of the ground. God gives man a body.

(3). <u>God's Breath</u> - Genesis 2:7b - And breathed into his nostrils the breath of life; and man became a living soul. God gives man a soul.

B. Three represents the three dimension of man: Spirit, Body and Soul.
C. Three represents the three psyche of man: Id, Ego and Super-ego.
D. Three represents the three spiritual purposes of man: Priest, Prophet, and King.
E. Three represents the devil's three strategies against man: John 10:10 "He comes to steal, kill and destroy."
F. Three represents the three female spirits assigned to attack the three-fold nature of man (His body, soul & spirit), the psyche of man (His Id, Ego & Superego) and the God directed purpose of man (His priestly office, prophetic office and his kingship). These three evil demonic girls are Delilah, Jezebel, and Athaliah.

One of the devil's strategies to bring mankind into captivity is to use these three female spirits to destroy God's original design for man holistically.

The Spiritual Realm

What is the spiritual realm? It is the unseen world, the invisible world (which is the real world). The original world was spirit and still is spirit. God is spirit and He occupies a spirit world.

> 2 Corinthians 4:18   While we look not at the things which are seen, but at the things which are not seen: for the things which are seen are temporal; but the things which are not seen are eternal.

Everything that exists naturally already existed in the spirit world. God spoke some things that had already existed in the spirit world into the natural world. Man was created in the Spiritual realm first. He was created in God's image and God's likeness. God did not speak the angels, the four little beasts or His beloved Son into the natural world.

Thank God, the Son, Jesus Christ the anointed one, came up under the new covenant, because we needed a Savior, a redeemer and a deliverer.

> Genesis 1:26a   And God said, Let us make man in our image, after our likeness.

God's image is spirit, on the sixth day man was created as a spirit being only. He was created in God's image, a spirit only. The first dimension of man that was created was his spirit. The bible says everything that God had made was finished by the sixth day. On the seventh day God rested. Man had been created as a spirit being, having God's likeness and image. Man was created with God's form and moral attributes. Man is a tri-fold being, spirit, body and soul. On the sixth day of creation, man possessed the spirit aspect of his three-fold nature.

God gave the man Adam a charge, to be fruitful, to multiply, to replenish the earth, to subdue it and take dominion over it. Adam could not carry out the charge of taking dominion over a natural world, with himself being spirit only. On the sixth day of creation, man's spirit was created and man knew God in the spirit. On the sixth day when God created Adam, he created him as male with female in him. She was there, but Eve had not yet been manifested.

> Genesis 1:26b — and let them have dominion over the fish of the sea, and over the fowl of the air, and over the cattle, and over all the earth, and over every creeping thing that creepeth upon the earth.

God blessed them and gave them their charge in the spirit first.

Genesis 1:27 -28 So God created man in his own image, in the image of God created he him; male and female created he them. And God blessed them, and God said unto them be fruitful, and multiply, and replenish the earth, and subdue it: and have dominion over the fish of the sea, and over the fowl of the air, and over every living thing that moveth upon the earth.

God deals with us from the inside-out. We come to know God in the spirit realm first and through our spirit, we fellowship with God. God blesses us in the spirit realm first, and he then implement, it in the natural realm.

Genesis 2:1 Thus the heavens and the earth were finished, and all the host of them.

Genesis chapter two, deals with the manifestation of man's body and soul created in the natural realm, to implement God's charge to them.

Genesis 2:5b for the Lord God had not caused it to rain upon the earth, and there was not a man to till the ground.

There was not a man, his body and soul was created in chapter 2. After the first seven days, Adam being a spirit man, could not take care of the earth naturally. So God formed him a natural, earthly body, so that he could implement the charges He gave unto them.

> Genesis 2:7 — And the Lord God formed man of the dust of the ground, and breathed into his nostrils the breath of life; and man became a living soul.

The second aspect of man's three fold nature that was created was man's body. God formed man's body from the dust of the ground. Man's flesh, his body, was made from dirt. Because man's flesh is from this world, man is in constant and continuous attacks from the temptations of this world and the temptations of women.

> 1 John 2:16 — For all that is in the world, the lust of the flesh, and the lust of the eyes, and the pride of life, is not of the father, but is of the world.

Paul says in Roman 7:18 For I know that in me (that is, in my flesh) dwelleth no good thing: for to will is present with me; but how to perform that which is good I find not.

Man's spirit is in constant battle with his body to live holy and righteous. There is a conflict because the body desires the things of this world and the spirit desires the things of God.

Paul says in Roman 7:24 O wretched man that I am! who shall deliver me from the body of this death?

The third aspect of man's three-fold nature is his soul. God breathe into him and gave him life. God gave man his essence. Man was now a spiritual and natural living soul.

II. Man's Three Fold Nature

In my study on spiritual warfare and my experience of casting out demons. I've noted that demons are released to attack the three fold nature of man.

I. Demonic Attacks Commissioned to Man's Spirit Nature

A. Demonized

As I stated earlier man's spirit nature was created first. This dimension of man deals with the spiritual realm and is the part of man that knows God and can fellowship with God. It is the God conscious part of man. Satan sends out an assignment via his demons to attack the spirit of man. There are men who are possessed by demonic spirits.

These spirits hold the spirit of man in captivity. These men which are afflicted may have a desire to know God and fellowship with God, but their spirit is held bound by satanic captivity. At time these men will act out religiously and they can become hostile, violent and aggressive. As in the 5th chapter of Mark, where a man was possessed by a legion of demons. The anointing of God can set a demonized victim free.

> Isaiah 61:1   The spirit of the Lord God is upon me; because the Lord hath anointed me to preach good tidings unto the meek; he hath sent me to bind up the brokenhearted, to proclaim liberty to the captives, and the opening of the prison to them that are bound.

> Isaiah 10:27b   and the yoke shall be destroyed because of the anointing.

Spiritual warfare (of binding and loosing) can set a demonized victim free.

> Matthew 18:18   Verily I say unto you, whatsoever ye shall bind on earth shall be bound in heaven: and whatsoever ye shall loose

on earth shall be loosed in heaven.

First of all we must recognize who we are in Christ Jesus. We are seated in heavenly places and we are joint heirs with Christ and he has given us the authority to bind and loose in his name on this earth.

B. Gigantism

Satan tried to alter the image and likeness of man by commissioning some of his fallen angels the nephilims to marry the daughters of men. This union altered the image and likeness of man by creating offspring that were half demonic angels and half human beings, which resulted into gigantism. A creature God never created. Satan has always tried to emulate the plan of God in a perverted way.

Genesis 6:1-4 And it came to pass, when men began to multiply on the face of the earth, and daughters were born unto them, That the sons of God saw the daughters of men that they were fair; and they took them wives of all which they chose. And the LORD said, My spirit shall not always strive with man, for that he also is flesh: yet his days shall be an hundred and twenty years.

Three Occult Female Spirits

There were giants in the earth in those days; and also after that, when the sons of God came in unto the daughters of men, and they bare children to them, the same became mighty men which were of old, men of renown.

Numbers 13:33   And there we saw the giants, the sons of Anak, which come of the giants: and we were in our own sight as grasshoppers, and so we were in their sight.

2 Samuel 21:20   And there was yet a battle in Gath, where was a man of great stature, that had on every hand six fingers, and on every foot six toes, four and twenty in number; and he also was born to the giant.

C. Homosexuality

Another spirit that Satan sends out to pervert the image and likeness of man is homosexuality. His plan is to make man less like God's image and likeness. Satan knows homosexuality is against the plan of God for mankind. God did not create a half man and half woman.

Genesis 1:27	So God created man in his own image, in the image of God created he him; male and female created he them.

Jesus said I came not to condemn but save. If we believe God to save and heal, we must also believe God to deliver those who has been led into captivity of perversion. God did not call us to condemn but to pray and warfare for those who are held captive.

John 3:17	For God sent not his Son into the world to condemn the world; but that the world through him might be saved.
Isaiah 61:1	The Spirit of the Lord GOD is upon me; because the LORD hath anointed me to preach good tidings unto the meek; he hath sent me to bind up the brokenhearted, to proclaim liberty to the captives, and the opening of the prison to them that are bound;

Homosexuality is not the plan of God for his most precious creation mankind. For God so loved man, that he gave his only begotten son, so that mankind can have eternal life. Satan hates the relationship between God and man. He therefore commissions his heinous demon cervello to attack the spirit nature of man.

Three Occult Female Spirits

Leviticus 20:13 — If a man also lie with mankind, as he lieth with a woman, both of them have committed an abomination; they shall surely be put to death; their blood shall be upon them.

Leviticus 18:22 — Thou shalt not lie with mankind, as with womankind: it is abomination.

Romans 1:26 - 27 — For this cause God gave them up unto vile affections: for even their women did change the natural use into that which is against nature: And likewise also the men, leaving the natural use of the woman, burned in their lust one toward another; men with men working that which is unseemly, and receiving in themselves that recompence of their error which was meet.

In homosexuality the demon cervello attacks, possess and enslaves, the spirit nature of man with female manifestation which are projected through his body and soulish entity. Demons incarcerate his manhood, male characteristics, male qualities and place his male attributes in captivity. The demons pervert the male characteristics into female characteristics. The demons may or may not incarcerate his masculinity depending upon his choice of wanting to be a male or female in the homosexual relationship.

In lesbianism the demon cervello attacks, possesses and enslaves the spirit nature of the woman or the girl. The demonic spirit perverts and turns her away from the proper purpose and use of what God created her for. This attack also is to oppose the plan of God for the woman.

For God said in:

<u>Genesis 2:18</u> - And the Lord God said, it is not good that the man should be alone; I will make him an help meet for him.

<u>Genesis 2:22</u> - And the rib, which the Lord God had taken from man, made he a woman, and brought her unto the man.

<u>Genesis 2:23</u> - And Adam said, this is now bone of my bones, and flesh of my flesh: she shall be called Woman, because she was taken out of Man.

In lesbianism, the cervello demon attacks her spirit nature. She then demonstrates male manifestation through her body and soulish entity. Demons incarcerate her womanhood, female characteristics, female qualities and her female attributes and place them in captivity. The demons may or may not incarcerate her femininity, depending upon her choice of wanting to be the man or woman in the homosexual relationship. There are generational curses of homosexuality within some families' bloodline. Homosexuality can be transferred, as in transferred spirits. Little boy babies and little girl babies can receive a homosexual attack against their spirit nature before or after the birthing of the child.

In fetal development there are three stages:

The First Stage is called the germinal stage which marks the beginning of development in to a human being. The fetus basic body structures are formed at this stage and demonic attacks can affect the fetus flesh-nature. This stage is where the basic formation of the body or flesh-nature occurs.

The Second Stage is called the embryonic stage; this is where the fetus begins to develop body organs. The second trimester is the period of maturation of organs, particularly the brain, in preparation for basic survival. At this stage demonic attacks affect the soulish-nature of the fetus, which consist of it's mind, intellect, memory, emotions and imagination. At this stage pray against demonic spirits that come to steal, kill and destroy the unborn fetus soulish nature.

To warfare against attacks pray against mood disorders such as major depression and bipolar disorders. Pray against antisocial personality disorders that can make one a psychopath, or schizophrenic at this stage of the fetal development. Start breaking generational curses by using prayers that can be found in my first book Prayers for Spiritual Warfare.

The Third Stage is called the fetal stage, in this stage the sexual organs become complete in both male and female. This is the stage where demons can attack the spirit of the fetus. This period starts with the embryonic stage until the actual child birth. Generational curses of homosexuality or an effeminate spirit can destroy the unborn fetus natural sexual orientation and oppose the plan of God's purpose for that child.

After this baby is born, the devil will commission a second homosexual attack against the child during the psychosexual stage of development.

There are five stages: According to Sigmund Freud's Theory, quoted from "Introduction of Psychosexual stage of development".

- ➢ The first stage is the oral stage which is early infancy until the first 18 months of life.
- ➢ The second stage is anal which involves late infancy from 1 ½ to 3 years.
- ➢ The third stage is the phallic stage, early childhood, from 3 to 6 years. The phallic stage is a time when the infant's pleasure seeking is centered on the genitals. This is the stage of development where the devil can commission a second homosexual or effemi-

nate attack against a child. At this time you need to cover the child in prayer and break generational curses if there are some in your bloodline.
- The fourth stage is the latency stage. This period is from the middle to late childhood (from 6 year old to puberty).
- The fifth stage is the genital stage. The period from puberty through adulthood. This is where the individual has renewed sexual desires. The genital stage is where the third attack against a man or woman's spirit can happen. The devil tries to inject homosexual drives, thoughts and desires in the spirit of man. As I stated earlier the devil emulated the plan of God, using the number three, targeting man's three-fold nature to pervert it.

D. Effeminate

Another spirit the devil assigns to keep man defeated and not walking in his authority is the effeminate spirit. It's area of attack is man's spirit. This can also, be a generational curse among the male seed. As I stated in chapter one an effeminate man is marked by weakness, and he can be a man that is soft, delicate and extremely gentle but this man is not necessarily homosexual. Satan's plan for an effeminate man is to keep him in a weak and passive state, never to be strengthened and never to mount up. The plan is to keep his confidence and self-worth low, to keep him from carrying out the charge that God gave him.

>Genesis 1:26a And God said, Let us make man in our image, after our likeness: and let them have dominion over all the earth.

E. Bestiality

Bestiality is another demonic attack that has been assigned to the spirit nature of mankind. There are many people living an alternative lifestyle with animals. These folks are called Zoophiles. These are people that have a personal intimate relationship with animals. They embrace a deep connection with their animals to the point of having sex with them. They view their animal as a spiritually equal. When God created, he created everything to mate and produce after it's own kind. God forbids intercourse between men and animals for this is perversion.

>Leviticus 18:23 And you shall not lie with any animal and so make yourself unclean with it, neither shall any woman give herself to an animal to lie with it: it is perversion.

>Leviticus 20:15 - 16 And if a man lie with a beast, he shall surely be put

to death: and ye shall slay the beast. And if a woman approach unto any beast, and lie down thereto, thou shalt kill the woman, and the beast: they shall surely be put to death; their blood shall be upon them.

Chapter 3

The Unveiling

Mark 4:22   For there is nothing hid, which shall not be manifested; neither was any thing kept secret, but that it should come abroad.

There is a familiar cliché that states, "what's done in the dark will come to the light". Man's three fold nature, (Spirit, body, and soul), the psyche of man (Id, Ego, and Superego), and the three spiritual purposes of man (Priest, Prophet, and King) have been under attack since Genesis the third chapter. Satan planned a diabolical occultic trick against man; bringing him into a spiritual, emotional and physical death. As long as Satan's plan is in the unknown he can operate and prevail against man's three fold nature, three fold psyche and will continue to assassinate the three spiritual purposes of man.

Many men from all walks of life are held in captivity by demonic spirits. Satan has assigned three female spirits to target man's three-fold nature, his three fold psyche and his three fold spiritual purpose, which God had ordained for man since his creation. God (Satan's former God and creator) had now created man in his likeness and image and Satan had a major problem with this, because God not only made us in His image, but he also gave man authority over this world which he once ruled.

For centuries Satan has operated behind the scene, using three female spirits to destroy the man that God made in his likeness and image. Remember as I stated earlier that Satan will also commission these spirits to oppress and possess the male gender. Satan sent out a pernicious, hideous, (but attractive attack) by using the woman. The very being that was created from him. Demons are real and they have been commissioned to bring man to his spiritual destruction, so that he will not accomplish his destiny which God had designed for his life.

Ephesians 6:12	For we wrestle not against flesh and blood, but against principalities, against powers, against the rulers of the darkness of this world, against spiritual wickedness in high places.

Man is not always enticed or captured because of flesh and blood. This thing is spiritual and it is in fact a spiritual battle.

> 2 Corinthians 2:14   Now thanks be unto God, which always causeth us to triumph in Christ, and maketh manifest the savour of his knowledge by us in every place.

The purpose of this book, is for men and women to receive their deliverance through reading and digesting this divine revelation that has been inspired by God through me. I pray that you will recognize these female spirits and others and be set at liberty from them, but before these spirits are unveiled I urge you to take a moment to both meditate and pray this prayer.

Father, God in the Name of Jesus Christ. I bind, I renounce and break myself from every un-teachable, and unlearned spirit. I loose myself from not comprehending the mysteries of the kingdom. I decree every demonic spirit that has been assigned to my intellect is bound in the name of Jesus. I loose a teachable and learned spirit, even a spirit of comprehension in Jesus name. I decree that my eyes are open in Jesus name, so that I may see and understand the hidden mysteries and the tangible things in the spirit realm. I now seal myself with the word of God.

James 1:5-6   If any of you lack wisdom, let him ask of God, that giveth to all men liberally, and upbraided not; and it shall be given him. But let him ask in faith, nothing wavering.

Deuteronomy 29:29   The secret things belong unto the Lord our God: but those things which are revealed belong unto us and to our children for ever, that we may do all the words of this law.

Thank you Lord Jesus. Amen.

This secretive, hideous, diabolical attack that was commissioned to destroy mankind has finally been revealed. This book will bring deliverance to husbands, fathers, sons, boyfriends, wives, mothers, girlfriends and the men and women who may be oppressed or possessed by these three female spirits. The secret hideous act is finally revealed and is no longer something hidden. The word of God says, he that hath ears to hear, let him hear what the spirit of the Lord is saying. These female spirits are real and they are not to be taken lightly. They are strong, they have personalities, emotions, intelligence and they are as deadly as a venomous snake. They are to be considered as demonic terrorists commissioned to assassinate the male and female seed.

I label these three female spirits as having a 3-D effect upon the man or the woman that has been victimized.

Delilah	-	Devilish
Jezebel	-	Dominating
Athaliah	-	Deadly

Every aspect of man's three-fold nature (body, spirit & soul), his psyche (Id, ego & superego) and his spiritual purpose (priest, prophet & king) are under attack. Many people are victimized by these female demonic spirits because they have failed to look beyond flesh and blood. Men and women are being raped and molested by these female spirits spiritually and they are being robbed of their psyche. Many victims are tormented, have lost their identity, they have lost their self-worth and also many have lost their fighting power. They have been overcome by these demonic and sinister spirits.

Paul warns the brethren in Ephesians 6 chapter, to be strong in the Lord and in the power of his might. He tells the brethren to put on the whole armor of God, that ye may be able to stand against the wiles of the devil. (The tricks of these she-devils).

> Ephesians 6:12   For we wrestle not against flesh and blood, but against principalities, against powers,

against the rulers of the darkness of this world, against spiritual wickedness in high places.

Paul further states that this is not a flesh and blood battle but it is spiritual, dealing with the spiritual, unseen world. In this verse, Paul also notes the four classes of demons. These three female spirits operates in the third class, they are ruling demons, (the strongman).

THREE FEMALE SPIRITS

II. Demonic Attacks Commissioned to Man's Flesh Nature

Man's flesh nature is constantly under attack. Man is often held in bondage by principalities, powers, rulers and spiritual wickedness in high places. There are men that are gifted, but yet bound. Men who are intelligent but bound and cannot maintain a job. Men with low self esteem that use other vices to conceal their true nature.

Men that lack self confidence are often times in need of constant stroking of their ego. But Jesus came to set the captives free. After God created man's spirit, He formed his body from the dust of the ground. This dimension of man deals in the physical realm and is the house in which we live.

Three Occult Female Spirits

> II Corinthians 5:1   For we know that if our earthly house of this tabernacle (body) were dissolved, we have a building of God, a house not made with hands, (spirit) eternal in the heavens.

Satan assigns demons to attack man's flesh nature. The purpose is to keep man in bondage to prevent him from fulfilling the purpose God has ordered for his creation. All sickness are not naturally caused by an illness or a disease that enters the body. There are illnesses and infirmities that are induced by demons. Demonic spirits are often assigned to inflict pain and trauma.

When there is no diagnosed medical reasons for an illness. Implement prayer for deliverance from a suspected demonic attack. Next, make a spiritual evaluation to determine what has oppressed or possessed your flesh nature.

> Matthew 7:16   Ye shall know them by their fruits.

Be careful to look for the strongman and his manifestation, then implement spiritual interventions. A strongman is a ruling demon that has the jurisdiction over a victim's body and life. Interventions like spiritual warfare, binding and loosing, prophetically praying, spiritual cleansing, fasting and praying (for further understanding of the words of terms included in the last sentence, turn to chapter 1 "Definition and Concepts").

> Luke 6:18   And they that were vexed with unclean spirits: and they were healed.
>
> Luke 4:40 - 41   Now when the sun was setting, all they that had any sick with divers diseases brought them unto him: and he laid his hands on every one of them, and healed them, and devils also came out of many, crying out, and saying, Thou art Christ the Son of God. And he rebuking them suffered them not to speak: for they knew that he was Christ.

Satan assigns spirits of infirmity to man's flesh nature. Sometimes there are demonic attacks that are launched out to attack the voice of a man and to keep him from speaking the oracles of God. All speech impediments are not natural, or disease inflicted.

> Matthew 9:32 - 33   As they went out, behold, they brought to him a dumb man possessed with a devil. And when the devil was cast out, the dumb spake: and the

multitudes marveled, saying, It was never so seen in Israel.

Demonic attacks have also been sent on assignment to attack man's vision. Not all eye diseases are from the natural aging process. There are demonic spirits that cause blindness.

Matthew 12:22   Then was brought unto him one possessed with a devil, blind, and dumb: and he healed him, insomuch that the blind and dumb both spake and saw.

Chapter 4

"cold hearted" "seductive"
"personal gain" "deceitful"
"sexy" "liar"
"trifling" "high esteem"
"sophisticated" "confident"
"persuasive" "cunning"

"agent to promote death"

The Female Spirit Delilah

Proverbs 6:24 - 26   To keep thee from the evil woman, from the flattery of the tongue of a strange woman. Lust not after her beauty in thine heart, neither let her take thee with her eyelids. For by means of a whorish woman a man is brought to a piece of bread: and the adulteress will hunt for the precious life.

King Solomon had extensive experience with women. He had 500 wives and 1000 concubines. God gave Solomon wisdom and he is known as the wisest man that's ever lived. In Solomon's old age, he had the wisdom, knowledge, understanding and life experience to impart wisdom into his son, on the subject of women. In Proverbs 6:24 - 26, Solomon warns his son to keep away from the spirit of Delilah.

Solomon was wise enough to see beyond her flattery and her beauty and he discerned that it was Delilah in operation. So many men today are captivated by the seductive, delicate, and the sensuous words that flow from a woman's lips which she has prepared primarily for him. She uses her luscious lips and her soft spoken voice to demonstrate or send her message to the man. When she uses her lips and her seductive eyes on a man often he will melt. The spirit of Delilah can seduce a man and bring him down to nothing.

Solomon's seven warning to men, regarding the spirit of Delilah.

| Delilah's flattering words - | Proverbs 7:5 - That they may keep thee from the strange woman, from the stranger |

	which flatterth with her words.
Delilah is crafty & cunning - (She dresses to allure men)	Proverbs 7:10 - And, behold, there met him a woman with the attire of an harlot, and subtile of heart.
Delilah is sexually aggressive - (Her approach is bold)	Proverbs 7:13-14 So she caught him, and kissed him, and with an impudent face said unto him, I have peace offerings with me; this day have I paid my vows.
Delilah informs him of the sensuous setting for sex - (She invites him over to her bedchamber)	Proverbs 7:16 -18 -I have decked my bed with coverings of tapestry, with carved works, with fine linen of Egypt.

I have perfumed my bed with myrrh, aloes, and cinnamon. Come, let us take our fill of love until the morning: let us solace ourselves with loves.

Delilah is persuasive - (She flatters him)

Proverbs 7:21 - With her much fair speech she caused him to yield, with the flattering of her lips she forced him.

Delilah traps him -

Proverbs 7:22 - 23 - He goeth after her straightway, as an ox goeth to the slaughter, or a fool to the correction of the stocks. Till a dart strike through his liver: as a bird hasteth to the snare, and knoweth not that it is for his life.

Solomon's Final Warning - Proverbs 7:25 - 27 - Let not thine heart decline to her ways, go not astray in her paths. For she hath cast down many wounded: yea many strong men have been slain by her. Her house is the way to hell, going down to the chambers of death.

HER MANIFESTATIONS

The spirit of Delilah attacks men of all classes, abilities and from all different walks of life. Delilah means beautiful, the dainty one or delicate. She is intriguing, deceitful, seductive, cold hearted, and she is a liar. The spirit of Delilah is trifling, and her goal is to obtain personal gain. She uses her feminity to gain money, power and fame.

She is not concerned about what cost comes from it or the damage it may bring. She will cause a man's relationship with God, his wife, his family and his nation, to deteriorate. She is beautiful and charming, but she has the poison of a rattle snake within her veins. The spirit of the python is in her arms, and she will crush him to death. She uses her physical charm, her body, her voice and her touch to lure a man to his spiritual and physical destruction.

Delilah is devilish and persuasive. She toys with a man's emotion, a Godly man's anointing, and with the status of a man in power. She deceives a man, causing him to believe she loves him. This hideous, diabolic spirit is the devil's prostitute. Under all that beauty and charm is the she-devil.

This heartless, pernicious spirit will bring any man down. Delilah is crafty and cunning, she studies her victims weakness before she attacks him just as a cat studies and charms a bird until it falls as it's prey. Delilah is known as the woman who brought down the powerful man Samson. The spirit of Delilah attacks men of power and authority and seeks to destroy a man. Delilah is a female ruling demon that has been assigned specifically to demonize the man's body and his Id.

She will steal his money, his relationship, his character and even his self worth. She is a trifling, cunning and calculating female spirit, who uses her sexuality for personal gain and to advance in the world as she knows it. The Delilah's spirit, stalks athletes, men in political positions, men in ministry, professional business men, and in general any man to receive personal gain.

Delilah Targets the Man's Body (flesh nature):

According to John 10:10a, the devil reveals Delilah's operational strategy is to steal. "The thief cometh not, but for to steal, and to kill, and to destroy".

Satan commissions the spirit of Delilah, a seductive she-devil, to target the man's body, his flesh and his sexual nature. The same body which is the temple of God. The same body which God desires man to present to him.

Roman 12:1	I beseech you therefore, brethren, by the mercies of God, that ye present your bodies, a living sacrifice holy, acceptable unto God, which is your reasonable service.

This flesh nature of man wants to be pleased by the lust of the flesh, the lust of the eyes and the pride of life. This seducing thief uses her body to entice men to lust for sexual gratification. Her game plan, as I have said before, is to steal his relationship from God, his wife and family.

Delilah Targets the Man's Id:

This cunning she-devil steals the Id of the man, the component of his personality that wants instant and pleasurable gratification. She is there to quench his sexual needs. Her goal is to deceive him by giving him his immediate sexual desire. Delilah has a game plan and her game plan is to demote him and disqualify his character. The spirit of Delilah is a tormenting spirit, she's constantly taunting a man until he is weaken. She will bring a man down to his lowest point just to be gratified.

Delilah Targets the Man's Priestly Position:

Delilah, is a thief. She steals the male seed from reigning as Priest. She will steal the anointing of a man of God. She works to stimulate the Godly male's libido, which in turn will pollute his priestly office. It was the spirit of Delilah which targeted the son's of Eli.

1 Samuel 2:22	Now Eli was very old, and heard all that his sons did unto all Israel: and how they lay with the women that assembled at the door of the tabernacle of the congregation.

Don't look now Delilah, but you have been exposed, your secret is out and it's not Victoria's secret.

Samson and Delilah Syndrome

Many men from the moment they are conceived within their mother's wombs are anointed, for a specific purpose, and this is ordained by God for their lives. From the beginning of time there have been demonic attacks launched out against the male seed. These demonic assignments were given to terminate the purpose of God's creation man. Man's purpose from the beginning has been to walk and live in the image and likeness of God and to have dominion upon the earth. Man was to be blessed, fruitful, multiply, and both replenish and subdue the earth.

God loves man and desires to have man's fellowship with him and have man's worship. As I stated earlier, Satan hates this unique relationship that man has with God and envies this relationship realizing this kind of fellowship is what he once shared with

God. Let's consider the Samson and Delilah syndrome. Samson was a Nazarene from birth.

A Nazarene is a person set apart for God's service. The vow of a Nazarene was one of abstinence from consuming alcohol, to refrain from cutting their hair, to avoid eating anything unclean or touching dead bodies, and to maintain a consecrated life before God.

Judges 13:4 – 5	Now therefore beware, I pray thee, and drink not wine nor strong drink, and eat not any unclean thing: For, lo, thou shalt conceive, and bear a son: and no razor shall come on his head; for the child shall be a nazarite unto God from the womb: and he shall begin to deliver Israel out of the hand of the Philistines.

Samson was physically strong because God anointed him with supernatural strength. He was a man of power and one of Israel's judges that reign for 20 years. The judges were military and civil leaders, who were to deliver the Israelites from foreign oppressors and to rule the people. Samson was a man of position and power. He fought many battles against the philistines with only his hands.

He removed gigantic iron gates of a city and carried them on his shoulders. He slew 1000 philistines all by himself using for a weapon the jawbone of a donkey. He killed a lion with his bare hands and he also set the philistines fields on fire ruining their crops. Samson did all these works under the supernatural power of the anointing that rested within his vows to God, being dedicated from birth by his mom, and by the Nazarene vow not to cut his hair.

Morally, Samson was weak. He violated all the nazarites vows. He drank wine, he ate grapes, he touched a dead body, when he wasn't suppose to, and he did not dedicate himself totally to God. After breaking all these vows, Samson maintained his anointing for physical strength because he had not revealed the secret of his strength.

But he could not fight his flesh of desiring strange attractive women. He could kill lions, but he couldn't kill his lust. His body dominated him with sensual and sexual desires. Samson had a very strong libido, which lead him to betrayal. Samson could break chains and bonds, but he could not break the bondage of his lust.

Samson slept with prostitutes night after night. Beautiful women distracted him from his mission. Spiritually, he was disobedient, and broke all the nazarite vows. This toying with his anointing lead him to his destruction. Samson was a man that functioned by his id. He was controlled by his flesh and he wanted sexual gratification.

Whatever he wanted, he had to have it right then in an instance. That's how he chose his first wife a philistine in an instance. Samson did not consider the consequences.

> Judges 14:2 – 4
>
> And he came up, and told his father and his mother, and said, I have seen a woman in Timnath of the daughters of the Philistines: now therefore get her for me to wife. Then his father and his mother said unto him, Is there never a woman among the daugthers of thy brethren, or among all my people,that thou goest to take a wife of the unircumcised Philistines? And Samson said unto his father, Get her for me; for she pleaseth me well. But his father and his mother knew not that it was of the Lord, that he sought an occasion against the Philistines: for at that time the Philistines had dominion over Israel.

Samson was controlled by his Id, which is about pleasure seeking and his drive was to satisfy his sexual needs. Because Samson was ruled by his Id, the pleasure principle of his psyche, he lived to satisfy his drives (sexually) and had no spiritual restrictions. Samson was selfish and he disobeyed the nazarite vows. Samson was a fierce enemy and brought crushing defeats continually to the philistines. The philistines could not over take him and neither were the philistines any match for Samson.

The philistines were ruled by five rich and powerful men, from five different cities. Delilah was a beautiful, seductive, cold hearted and calculating philistine woman who lived in the valley of Sorek. Her reputation seem to be as a woman who would do what she had to do, to get what she wanted which was money and power. She had no remorse regarding the men she brought low. One day these five powerful men, (men of authority and rulership) learned that Samson was in love with this ruthless woman.

These men of power came to Delilah and asked her to entice Samson, and find out where his strength lieth, so that they may bind and afflict him. They offered to pay her richly for her betrayal. This ruthless female spirit delivered Samson into the philistines hands. Delilah's spirit worked on his pleasure principals. She gave him sexual satisfaction, but it came with a high price.

This devilish she-devil, with rattle snake venom on her lips and the arms of a python continued to entice him daily to find the secret of his strength. Finally Samson grew weak and gave in, and he revealed to Delilah where his secret lieth. Samson was lying in her lap when she cut his hair and he lost his strength. Men, what's in a strange woman's lap? The very thing that can bring pleasure can also be destructive.

Judges 16:19   And she made him sleep upon her knees: and she called for a man, and she caused him to shave off the seven locks of his head: and she began to afflict him, and his strength went from him.

Men are being raped from their masculinity sexually by the influence of demonic powers. The devil uses some women to be the aggressor sexually (most men love to have women that are sexually aggressive) and that could be ok some times. But it could have some hidden adverse reactions. The more men indulge into this type of relationship, he might become passive, docile and look up toward the woman in the bed chamber. He might then start to demonstrate passiveness which could open up a door to be dominated by females.

This can be an open door for the dominatrix to walk in because she has dominated him sexually and she could then seek to dominate other aspects of his life. She can dominate him physically, emotionally and spiritually, if he allows her to dominate him in the bedchamber. The adverse reaction is it could help to destroy his manhood, and eventually he takes on the spirit of Ahab. The bible says "a man that find a wife, findeth a good thing". The husband is the hunter and he should take his position and authority as the king of the jungle in the bedchamber.

Delilah dominated Samson in the bedchamber, he lost his authority and power and this opened up the area of him not seriously regarding his anointing.

Judges 16:10 - 17   And Delilah said unto Samson, Behold, thou hast mocked me, told me lies: now tell me, I pray thee, wherewith thou mightest be bound. And he said unto her, If they bind me fast with new ropes that never were occupied, then shall I be weak, and be as another man. Delilah therefore took new ropes, and bound him therewith, and said unto him, The Philistines be upon thee, Samson. And there were liers in wait abiding in the chamber. And he brake them from off his arms like a thread. And Delilah said unto Samson, Hitherto thou hast mocked me, and told me lies: tell me wherewith thou mightest be bound. And he said unto her, If thou weavest the seven locks of my head with the web. And she fastened it with the pin, and said unto him, The Philistines be upon thee, Samson. And he

Three Occult Female Spirits

awaked out of his sleep, and went away with the pin of the beam, and with the web. And she said unto him, How canst thou say, I love thee, when thine heart is not with me? thou hast mocked me these three times, and hast not told me wherein thy great strength lieth. And it came to pass, when she pressed him daily with her words, and urged him, so that his soul was vexed unto death; That he told her all his heart, and said unto her, There hath not come a razor upon mine head; for I have been a Nazarite unto God from my mother's womb: if I be shaven, then my strength will go from me, and I shall become weak, and be like any other man.

In today's society there are many anointed men of God. They can fight in the midst of calamities and trials, but they are unable to control their fleshly desire for strange women. Many great anointed men of God, have broken their nazarite vows and toyed with their anointing, because of their desire for beautiful ungodly women. As I was mediating about the spirit of Delilah. Spiritually I saw her operating in high places.

This she-devil spirit that is in operation attacked a high political authority. Her goal was to bring down and assassinate the powerful man's character. Delilah operates in many woman who entice professional athletes and then cry rape. This she-devil targets men of all caliber who have been appointed and called to preach the gospel.

The book of Ecclesiastes informs us that there is nothing new under the sun. Everything that is existing now, had already existed before our time. Utilize this revelation knowledge and hide it within your heart.

> Ecclesiastes 1:9b - 10 And there is no new thing under the sun. Is there anything wherest it may be said, see, this is new? It hath been already of old time, which was before us.

Chapter 5

The Female Spirit of Jezebel

Multiple Personality Disorder: Female and Male

Signs, Symptoms and Manifestations of the spirit of Jezebel

Dominating	Rebellion
Controlling	Convert
Intimidation	Un-submitted
Manipulation	Witch
Divination	Warlock
Perversion	Unrepentant
Arrogant	Liar
Cold Hearted	Hate
Calculating	Emasculate Men
Possessive	Dictator
Sows Discord	Power Hungry
Project Fear	Aggressive

Ruthless
Undermines Authority

Idolatry
Jealousy

I Kings 19: 2 - 3

Then Jezebel sent a messenger unto Elijah, saying so let the gods do to me, and more also, if I make not thy life as the life of one of them by tomorrow about this time. And when he saw that, he arose, and went for his life, and came to Beer-sheba, which belongth to Judah, and left his servant there.

II Kings 9:22

And it came to pass, when Joram saw Jehu, that he said, Is it peace, Jehu? And he answered, what peace, so long as the whoredom of thy mother Jezebel and her witchcrafts are so many?

History of Jezebel

The second female spirit that is on an assignment is the spirit of Jezebel. She is a bi-gender dominating witch or warlock spirit that can resident in both female and male. Jezebel is known as a prideful, non-repented, dictator and tyrant. Her mission is to destroy the spirit gender of the male or female along with the ego and also destroy their spiritual leadership as a Prophet. Jezebel was actually a psychopath, who suffered multiple personality disorders.

She was a very aggressive woman who also was violent, and demonstrated anti-social thoughts and behavior. She was the daughter of King Ethbal, who was involved in pagan worship, perversion and divination. Jezebel was raised in an environment of licentious sexual acts, Sodomy and also idolatry. This type of lifestyle was the conduit to her tapping into the powers of darkness and demon-gods, (which they worshipped). These gods were also connected with Baal and Ashtoroth (goddess of love, lust and sensuality) which also promoted animal and child sacrifices, perversion, ritualistic and sensual dancing, as well as Sodomy by male and female prostitutes.

Jezebel transformed from being a psychopath princess to a demonic outraged queen whore over Israel, by marrying King Ahab. Finally, she became the queen mother giving birth to her daughter Althaliah, who was, as hard as it is to believe, more ruthless than her mother Jezebel. Althaliah, tried to sabotage the kingdom from the inside by killing off her grandsons while Jezebel tried to destroy spiritual leaders' from the outside by killing the prophets. In the Hebrew language, the name Jezebel means "without cohabitation". This spirit will not exist or co-habit with those he or she cannot control or dominate.

I Kings 16:31B	"that he took to wife Jezebel the daughter of Ethbaal king of the Zidonians, and went and served Baal, and worshipped him".

The Spirit of Jezebel Destroys the Ego

The spirit of Jezebel is a spirit that commissions a three-fold attack to invade and demoralize the ego, along with the spirit and spiritual office of a prophet. According to Dr. Siqmumd Freud's structural model of the psyche, the ego is one of the three components of a person psyche. It is viewed as the organized and realistic part of the man or woman's psyche. The ego is a person's view or personal idea of their self worth or importance. Jezebel intimidates and dominates the man's ego until she destroys it and he no longer values his self worth or importance.

She works to destroy his manhood by converting him to a wimp or an effeminate boy or man (which can be a door to a homosexual spirit). Jezebel will sentence the male seed to what I call the Ahab syndrome. The Ahab syndrome is like king Ahab. It's where a man is both emasculated and totally passive and under her control. She has both incarcerated and castrated many men and women by transforming them from their natural state by transforming them as her eunuchs.

Globally the spirit of Jezebel still sits upon her throne reigning as queen mother in high places, castrating and retarding the development of both men and women. While she is demasculating the male seed she also defeminize the female seed.

II Timothy 3:2 - 3	For men shall be lovers of their own selves, covetous, boasters, proud, blasphemers, disobedient to parents, unthankful, unholy, Without natural affection, trucebreakers, false accusers, incontinent, fierce, despisers of those that are good,

Jezebel's Eunuchs

The eunuchs of Jezebel's are visibly seen in female dominated marriages. The wife totally controls the marriage and does the speaking and interceding for the husband. She spiritually castrates him, thereby making him her eunuch. He is then demasculated as her covering and the head of the home. These husbands are the so called, "yes dear" husbands. She exerts her power over her husband by manipulating him through sex. The woman that is oppressed or possessed by Jezebel is a very cold hearted, self-centered woman.

She is concerned only about her happiness. The greater her ability to control men, the more empowered she feels. Jezebel's eunuchs are often hidden in domestic violence type relationships. She has castrated the egos of both men and women, damaging their self-esteem, through physical and emotional abuse. Leaving them in a state, whereas they are afraid to perform as healthy women or men having a positive outlook of themselves.

Leaving them with fear and low self-esteem where the abuse has been not just physically but also mentally. The ego has been castrated and now the victim feels worthless and lives with fear.

The Spirit of Jezebel tries to Destroy the Prophetic Office

I Kings 18:13   "Was it not told my Lord what I did when Jezebel slew the prophets of the Lord, how I hid a hundred men of the Lord's prophets by fifty in a cave and fed them with bread and water?"

The spirit of Jezebel is an arrogant, cold – hearted, and calculated sower of discord that tries to destroy the male or female seed from reigning as prophet. Her goal is to kill off the true prophets.

Knock Knock Jezzie, it's time to deal with you so stop the drama. Your game has come to an abrupt end. We prophetically decree the ancestral anointing of Jehu to trample over and destroy you.

This psychopath, is an undercover demonic witch or warlock that possesses different personalities. One of her personalities targets the prophetic office and will try to destroy spiritual leadership. She opposes true spiritual authority and will promote disciples to divorce themselves from their true spiritual leader through the spirit of divination.

She uses her energy to try and manipulate them out of their destiny. I spiritually diagnose this personality as Jezebel type I. Her assignment is to promote a loss of spiritual authority in the kingdom of God. She seduces the church to commit spiritual fornication by seduction and teachings of doctrines of devils. Enticing the church to lose God's vision by spiritually sleeping with false leadership.

Many churches have Jezebels sitting on thrones over their churches. This is the reason many churches have accepted sexual perversion amongst the disciples. Jezebel's eunuch are in leadership, safe guarding and protecting her. As she continues to worship and empower Asthorth, the goddess of lust, with perverted sexual acts. Now is the season to decree the ancestral anointing of Jehu to command her eunuchs to throw her out, so the demon dogs can devour her.

Personality type I, is empowered through the avenue of false prophecy's and false teaching. Prophecy that has not been directed by God and teachings that are not doctrinal or of God.

> Jeremiah 14:14 — Then the LORD said unto me, The prophets prophesy lies in my name: I sent them not, neither have I commanded them, neither spake unto them: they prophesy unto you a false vision and divination, and a thing of nought, and the deceit of their heart

> I Timothy 4:1 - 2 — Now the Spirit speaketh expressly, that in the latter times some shall depart from the faith, giving heed to seducing spirits, and doctrines of devils; Speaking lies in hypocrisy; having their conscience seared with a hot iron;

> Revelation 2:20 - 21 — Notwithstanding I have a few things against thee, because thou sufferest that woman Jezebel, which calleth herself a prophetess, to teach and to seduce my servants to commit fornication, and to eat things sacrificed unto idols. And I

gave her space to repent of her fornication; and she repented not.

The Personality type I of Jezebel is that of a spiritual and diabolical whore. Globally she is leading God's people into immorality with her false prophets and false doctrines. Jezebel is leading the people of God into sexual immorality and diluting the gospel with the sinful things of this world, by destroying their spirit nature or the spirit of God that lies within them.

This personality is assigned to assassinate the character of the men and women of God, directing them into a reprobated state. This is a place where the victims becomes morally depraved, wretched, wicked, corrupt, and without principles. Her goal is to massacre all true prophets and set up her high places, alters and groves. Her high places are set up with her false prophets, eunuchs, witches, warlocks and gods Baal and Asthorth.

II Kings 9:22b   And he answered, What peace, so long as the whoredoms of thy mother Jezebel and her witchcrafts are so many?

The Spirit of Jezebel Slander's Naboth

This spirit's goal is to slander the character of true men and women of God. One of the dark sides of Jezebel is when she coverts something, she also will slander it. Jezebel slandered Naboth, then had him murdered and stole his vineyard. This spirit is actively operating in the kingdom today. Folks are coveting Apostolic and pastoral ministries by slandering the men and women of God in order to bring death to their ministries and finally take over the vineyard, which is the congregation.

Those who's ministries have been under attack, need to declare and decree the ancestral anointing of Jehu. You can not play or entertain the Jezebel spirit. You must decree death to her, and command the dogs to consume her. This aspect of her personality is very nasty and evil.

I Kings 21:14 - 16	Then they sent to Jezebel, saying, Naboth is stoned, and is dead. And it came to pass, when Jezebel heard that Naboth was stoned, and was dead, that Jezebel said to Ahab, Arise, take possession of the vineyard of Naboth the Jezreelite, which he refused to give thee for money: for Naboth is not alive, but dead. And it came to pass, when Ahab heard that Naboth was

dead, that Ahab rose up to go down to the vineyard of Naboth the Jezreelite, to take possession of it.

Jezebel's Male Personality

The Jezebel spirit is a deranged female spirit with different personalities and genders. One gender is male. In the book of Genesis Laban, Jacob's uncle showed a Jezebel spirit. He manipulated, controlled and deceived Jacob for fourteen years. Laban's objective was to control and manipulate Jacob for his own financial gain and personal gratification.

> Genesis 29:25   And it came to pass, that in the morning, behold, it was Leah: and he said to Laban, What is this thou hast done unto me? did not I serve with thee for Rachel? wherefore then hast thou beguiled me?

There are many people in spiritual leadership, that have not been positioned by God. They are oppressed or possessed by Jezebel and seek self-gratification and greed. The prophetic office has always been under attack by the spirit of Jezebel. She hates the prophets because they speak the mind of God. Jezebel works to kill out the prophetic anointing of those who are seerers and also the vocal prophets.

She is threatened by true prophets who can see her false world system which she has set up globally over churches, nations, kingdoms and regions. Jezebel is threatened by those who can cause destruction to her influence as queen mother over many nations.

> I Kings 19:1 – 2   And Ahab told Jezebel all that Elijah had done, and withal how he had slain all the prophets with the sword. Then Jezebel sent a messenger unto Elijah, saying, So let the gods do to me, and more also, if I make not thy life as the life of one of them by to morrow about this time.

The spirit of Jezebel can also operate in spiritual leaders who have been called and ordained by God. Just because one has been anointed and consecrated in one of the five-fold ministry offices, he or she is not exempt from Jezebel's control. In fact Jezebel seeks those in leadership, and her purpose is to get them to abort their destiny. She figuratively feeds them her witches brew, intoxicating them into believing that they need not be subject to spiritual authority. After being drunken with her brew, they decide they don't have to submit, respect or consult the holy spirit or those that are in a higher level of authority.

King Saul, Israel's first king, whom God appointed and set up to lead his people, had a Jezebel spirit. He constantly disrespected and operated in disobedience to his spiritual authority, the prophet Samuel. He eventually became so ruthless and godless that he became a killer of God prophets. King Saul became so jealous of the anointing of David and the battles David had won, that he conspired against David and plotted to destroy him.

> I Samuel 15:9 - 11 But Saul and the people spared Agag, and the best of the sheep, and of the oxen, and of the fatlings, and the lambs, and all that was good, and would not utterly destroy them: but every thing that was vile and refuse, that they destroyed utterly. Then came the word of the LORD unto Samuel, saying, It repenteth me that I have set up Saul to be king: for he is turned back from following me, and hath not performed my commandments. And it grieved Samuel; and he cried unto the LORD all night.

> I Samuel 22:17 - 18 And the king said unto the footmen that stood about him, Turn, and slay the priests of the LORD: because their

hand also is with David, and because they knew when he fled, and did not shew it to me. But the servants of the king would not put forth their hand to fall upon the priests of the LORD. And the king said to Doeg, Turn thou, and fall upon the priests. And Doeg the Edomite turned, and he fell upon the priests, and slew on that day fourscore and five persons that did wear a linen ephod.

This same spirit came against the prophetic office of Moses and his ministry. Aaron and Miriam operated under the Jezebel and Ahab syndrome. The Jezebel spirit influenced them to say and believe that God, spoke to them as he did Moses. The spirit of Jezebel will come alive within the bloodlines of families that are called to ministry. She will manipulate the weaker vessels to come against the prime authority figure, that God has called and established in the family to bring deliverance, set-up structure, and to institute an apostolic government of order.

As people of God, we should never be consumed by outer appearances totally wrapped up in what you see visibly. The bible declares "for man looks at the outer appearance, but God looks at the heart". The spirit of Jezebel, which is a hater of the prophets, had John the Baptist imprisoned and decapitated, because he preached repentance, and about the kingdom coming. The spirit masqueraded herself in the form of Herodias.

> Mark 6:17, 22, 24
>
> For Herod himself had sent forth and laid hold upon John, and bound him in prison for Herodias' sake, his brother Philip's wife: for he had married her.
> (22) And when the daughter of the said Herodias came in, and danced, and pleased Herod and them that sat with him, the king said unto the damsel, Ask of me whatsoever thou wilt, and I will give it thee.
> (24) And she went forth, and said unto her mother, What shall I ask? And she said, The head of John the Baptist.

Jezebel has intoxicated many of the true prophets minds with her witches brew leaving them incapacitated with a dementia or schizophrenic spirit. Many of the true prophets have been enslaved or incarcerated with mental health diseases, subjecting them to medication and psychologist. Because these people can prophesy the mind of God, she works to destroy their mind leaving them to depend upon medication and become (if it were possible) walking zombies.

She disables them from hearing the voice of God. Many true prophets have been afflicted and have been relegated to the mental health ward.

Jezebel is a witch, that has lead many true prophets to prostitute their prophetic gifts in the area of divination. The spirit of Jezebel is continually trying to get the kingdom sons and daughters under her evil influence. Because she now recognizes that the apostolic sons and daughters are now advancing the kingdom of God, and the Father is unveiling new revelation. Her attacks have accelerated and we kingdom people now know that the kingdom of God is within us and we have the authority to govern all our adjacent territories.

There is an apostolic – prophetic decree that the ancestral anointing of Jehu's company of kingdom folks is coming forth to overthrow, Jezebel the demonic queen mother, who has been sitting upon her throne globally.

Revelation 2:20	Notwithstanding I have a few things against thee, because thou sufferest that woman Jezebel, which calleth herself a prophetess, to teach and to seduce my servants to commit fornication, and to eat things, sacrificed unto idols.

Jezebel Dominates Her Mate

Jezebel the bi-gender spirit, has a second personality and it's purpose is to dominate, and control her mate. I spiritually diagnose this personality as Jezebel type II. This is a spirit of divination, that is unsubmissive and cold-hearted toward his or her mate. Because she has multiple personalities, one of her personalities is constantly fighting the male seed for control and authority. She is self centered, selfish and seeks to control and manipulate her husband through sex.

The Spirit of Jezebel Destroys the Spirit of Man

1. Jezebel is a spirit that attacks man's spirit nature, conforming him into something God did not create him to be. She destroys his natural purpose as a man and her natural purpose as a woman. Transforming men into women and women into men. She destroys the image of God's original purpose.

"Let us make man in our image and likeness" - Genesis 1:26

2. Satan commissions the spirit of Jezebel this dominating witch to assassinate the spirit and image of God's original design for man and woman. That dimension of man, whereas God spoke and said

"Let us make man in our image and our likeness". She destroys his spirit and annihilates his relationship with God and his natural use as a man or woman. Man is the only being in the world that God created in His image and likeness. The spirit of Jezebel targets and destroys the spirit because this is the dimension of man that communes with God, and that comes into fellowship and relationship with God. Man's spirit being is where the Holy Spirit comes in and residents.

> I Kings 21:7 – 8   And Jezebel his wife said unto him, Dost thou now govern the kingdom of Israel? arise, and eat bread, and let thine heart be merry: I will give thee the vineyard of Naboth the Jezreelite. So she wrote letters in Ahab's name, and sealed them with his seal, and sent the letters unto the elders and to the nobles that were in his city, dwelling with Naboth.

Her purpose is to emasculate men from their spiritual and physical leadership.

3. We all know that, God is love and that he love everyone and also that we are all commissioned to love ye one another. We also know he created us in his image and likeness and God has commissioned us

to dominate, take authority, multiply and replenish the earth. Jezebel's assignment on the other hand, is to get man to abort the assignment given to men and women by God. God loves all people and gave his son so that we may have eternal life, but God also detest sin and unrighteousness.

Ephesians 6:12	For we wrestle not against flesh and blood, but against principalities, powers, against rulers of the darkness of this world, against spiritual wickedness in high places.
Romans 5:8	But God commendeth his love toward us, in that, while we were yet sinners, Christ died for us.
Romans 6:23	For the wages of sin is death; but the gift of God is eternal life through Jesus Christ our Lord.
John 3:16	For God so loved the world, that he gave his only begotten Son, that whosoever believeth in him should not perish, but have everlasting life.
1 John 4:8	He that loveth not knoweth not God; for God is love.

2 Peter 3:9	The Lord is not slack concerning his promise, as some men count slackness; but is longsuffering to us-ward, not willing that any should perish, but that all should come to repentance.

The Bi-gender Queen Mother Throneship

4. The spirit of Jezebel is bi-gender. She seeks to emasculate men and defeminize women. She promotes homosexuality and same sex marriage. Jezebel also, promotes down low activities (men operating as heterosexual but secretly operating as homosexuals), bestiality and all types of perversion. She establishes her throne in high places, in our society.

She establishes it in the political arena, the churches, the educational departments, sports athletes, Hollywood actors and the music industry. Jezebel mandates that her eunuchs protect her demonic doctrine and anyone that comes against her doctrine can be labeled as anti-homosexual, and as someone that discriminates.

Data Relating to Bi-Sexual Relationships

5. The bi-sexual Queen Mother's throneships are set up internationally.

I. Gay marriages are extended nationwide in Canada
By: Clifford Krauss
Published: June 29, 2005
Toronto, June 28 - The House of Common voted Tuesday night to extend marriage rights to gay and lesbian couples throughout Canada despite strong opposition from the Conservatives and a splintering of the governing Liberal Party Caucus.
   *Reference: Mytimes.com

II. Same sex marriages are currently granted by five of the 50 states, one federal district, and one Indian Tribe
In Connecticut, Iowa, Massachusetts, New Hampshire, Vermont and Washington DC, marriages for same sex couples are legal and currently performed. The coquille Indian Tribe in Oregon also grants same-sex marriage.
   *Reference: Wikipedia (the free encyclopedia)

III. Same sex marriage laws in the Netherlands
By: Ramon Johnson, About.com Gurde

04/01/01	-	The Netherlands becomes the first nation to legalize same-sex marriage.
11/30/06	-	South Africa became the fifth country, and the first in Africa, to legalize same-sex marriage.
12/09/04	-	Same-sex civil unions were introduced into law in New Zealand.
07/03/05	-	Spain legalizes same sex-marriage, becoming the third nation behind the Netherlands and Belgium to grant gay marriage.

Queen Mother Position's Her Throneship Over Churches

The Metropolitan community church or the Universal Fellowship of Metropolitan community churches is an international protestant Christian denomination. The fellowship has a specific outreach to lesbian, gay, bisexual and transgender families and communities.

*Reference: Wikipedia (the free encyclopedia)

The old Catholic Churches in Germany, Switzerland, Austria and the Netherlands view homosexuality as moral, and permits gay and lesbian priests, as well as blesses gay couples.

Chapter 6

Signs, Symptoms and Manifestations of the spirit of Athaliah

Dominating
Controlling
Intimidation
Manipulation
Divination
Murder (male seeds)
Desires Empowerment
Cold Hearted
Calculating
Aggressive
Mental Disorder

Rebellion
Un-submitted
Unrepentant
Ruthless
Jealousy
Idolatry
Liar
Hate
Dictator
Projects Fear

The Female Spirit of Athaliah

The third female spirit that Satan commissions is the spirit of Athaliah. We can call her the terminator for she is a female terrorist. Athaliah targets the soulish realm of the man. She is a cold-blooded and calculating spirit that kills the life in a man. The spirit of Athaliah murders the male seed both literally and physically. Regarding the literal, Athaliah targets the man's <u>super ego</u>.

She kills his aspirations and his prohibitions. This female terrorist reduces the male seed to a dead, defeated, apathic life style. The manifestation of physical death by this spirit can be seen in the many mothers that have killed their own sons. Athaliah will kill the male seed to prevent him from reigning in his <u>kingship</u>.

The clock has struck 12 midnight and just like Cinderella, Althaliah, you have been exposed. We prophetically decree that the male seeds shall live and not die, but declare the works of God.

Now according to John 10:10a, the devil reveals Althaliah's operational strategy, is to kill. "The thief cometh not but for to steal, and to kill, and to destroy". The spirit of Athaliah is the female terrorist assigned to kill the male seed's soulish realm, his super ego and destroy his kingship.

THE FEMALE SPIRIT ATHALIAH

As I was before the Lord, He revealed unto me this third pernicious female spirit. The Spirit of Athaliah, will literally kill the male seed and castrate him of his manhood. I am a person that loves nature, and I enjoy watching the discovery and animal planet channels. One evening as I was watching one of these channels, they featured the Tasmanian Devil. And I noted after the mating process, the female Tasmanian Devil demonstrated such a great hatred toward the male Tasmanian Devil that she was going to literally kill him if he didn't get out of that burrow or den (her place of authority).

Athaliah is just like the Tasmanian devil, she will kill her male counter part, if he does not get out of her place of authority. Athaliah can be known as the death spirit Sam(m)el assigned by satan to kill out the male seed. This spirit seduces the male seed. Her assignment is to both dominate him and kill him.

Unlike Jezebel, Athaliah does not plan or set up strategies on how to bring a man down or destroy his male hood. She just kills him point blank. That's why she is the terminator assigned to kill the male seed.

HISTORY OF ATHALIAH

Athaliah was the daughter of Ahab and Jezebel. She inherited the same genetic make-up as her mother Jezebel. After the death of her husband King Jehoram, her son Ahaziah became king. King Ahaziah was forty-two years old trying to reign as a king, and yet he was very childish and leaned to his mother to counsel him on how to reign as a man and a king. From childhood his mother Athaliah had spiritually castrated and killed his manhood by the control she had over him.

Listening to his mother Athaliah's counseling also helped him to turn God's people from God. Athaliah dominated her son and weakened his soulish realm, his mind, his emotions and his intellect until he was totally destroyed as a man. He was a mama's boy at forty-two years old. This spirit of Athaliah lives today in many women and they will not allow their sons, brothers or husbands to reign as the king that God has called them to be. This is the reason we have a generation of weak, worthless and ineffective men today.

Men that will never reign in their kingship. Some examples, are men who will not find or keep a job, don't put their family first, and won't take care of their children. Athaliah will stunt the growth of a man, keeping him in a childlike state, and totally dependent upon the female gender.

> 2 Chronicles 22:2 - 3 Forty and two years old was Ahaziah when he began to reign, and he reigned one year in Jerusalem. His mother's name also was Athaliah the daughter of Omri. He also walked in the ways of the house of Ahab: for his

mother was his counselor to do wickedly.

This woman lived during a time when Israel's kings and leadership disregarded the things of God and turned completely away from God. Athaliah grew up in an environment of a weak father and a dominating, pagan worshipping mother. She was surrounded with groves, idols of baal and people who continually worshiped pagan gods and not the true and only living God. Thus Athaliah denied the true God "Jehovah".

Today the spirit of Athaliah has come into empowerment, because the leaders of our country, have turned away from the true doctrines of God. Our country has opened doors to immorality and idolatry, and this has empowered the spirit of Athaliah. The more our country promotes immorality and idolatry, the more the spirit of Athaliah is being made manifest in our world. The spirit of Athaliah kills the male-seed sexuality. This is one reason for such an increase in homosexuality among the male-seed. Some times this queen-mother has intimidated the males testorone drive, preventing him from walking in his God given role as a male and as king.

Athaliah, the Territorial Spirit

Athaliah the queen-mother is a territorial ruling spirit. She is a spirit that controls either a territory consisting of land or people. Although King Ahaziah her son was king, Athaliah was actually the one that was the power behind the power. After her son was killed, Athaliah realized that her son's death would cause her to lose her position and power. She also knew that when her grandson would become king that his wife would become queen, and she the queen-mother would lose her position of power and riches.

This cold-hearted, woman murdered all of her grandsons (the male-seed) except for the one that was hidden. The spirit of Athaliah will murder her own male-seed for power and position.

> 2 Chronicles 22:10   But when Athaliah the mother of Ahaziah saw that her son was dead, she arose and destroyed all the seed royal of the house of Judah.

This spirit is definitely in operation today, manifesting itself by those killing off the male seed. This female spirit operates with the spirit of witchcraft, projecting manipulation, intimidation and domination against the male-seed. Athaliah is an arrogant female spirit that is jealous of her own seed. She does not grieve the lost of her sons or grandsons. She seeks an opportunity for self-empowerment.

Her jealousy is strong and dominates her, until she is driven to kill off the male seed. She will murder anything that will prevent her from achieving her position of authority. The spirit of Athaliah operates in abortion clinics, feminist movements, lesbianism, hollywood movies and other areas where women are killing the male seed.

The Three Dimension of Man
(Soulish realm under attack (Athaliah attacks the soul) of the man)

The three dimension of man are body, spirit and soul. The spirit of Athaliah directly attacks the soulish realm of the man. Within the soulish realm, five entities are housed. The will, emotion, intellect, imagination and memory. This spirit's assignment is to kill his will. The spirit of Athaliah is like cancer it will eat away his desires to achieve and destroy any of his aspirations. He will have no desire to walk in his God given role as a man. In fact he will be too weak, because Athaliah has emasculated him from his role as a man. This spirit hampers him in his efforts of leadership in his home, community and also in his relationship with God. She totally overwhelms him until the man has no desire or little will power in establishing a relationship with God.

This man will go through life being unaccountable. Because his will, has been attacked by the spirit of Athaliah. In today's society we have too many men that are indecisive in matters, regarding their life, their family and their relationship with God. Men that have no desire to walk in their purpose or reach their God directed destiny, bringing him into a somewhat worthless state. The spirit of Athaliah kills his desire to be productive as well as his emotions, delivering him into an apathetic state.

This results in him having no or little concern for God, his family and even himself. With a lack of will these men can be comfortable with being homeless. They also can become comfortable institutionalized in the prison system where their decisions are already made for them. This spirit can cause the male-seed to commit homicide or suicide.

Demonic attacks commissioned to man's soulish - nature

When man received the breath of life from God, the third dimension of man was created and he became a living person. This is the soulish realm of man and it consist of his will/mind, his emotions, his intellect, imagination and his memory. Satan's greatest attack against the three fold-nature of man, is the man's soulish realm. Here is where he sends out demonic attacks against the different components of the soulish realm. Some demonic attacks against the mind/will of man, can lead him to live in disobedience to God.

He either will not want to covenant with God or he is unable to choose to covenant with God because of a demonic attack against his decision making process. Satan attacks man's emotions by sending attacks against his emotion often times causing the man to feel either self pity, arrogance, anger, low self-esteem, being defensive or depressed. It also can make him feel despair, hopelessness or suicidal tendencies. Satan sends out an attack against man's intellect, and can cause him to be illiterate, unteachable, lacking wisdom, and unable to reason. Satan attacks the man's thinking ability.

He attacks man's imagination with demonic attacks that causes him to have hallucinations and delusions. There are demonic spirits that cause him to be schizophrenic and have phobias or procrastinate and become a compulsive liar and this will affect his visions, goals and ideas. Another area that satan sends attacks against man is in his memory causing him to have OBS, Alzheimer or possibly amnesia. This area is where man's mental recall center lies.

1 Peter 2:11	Dearly beloved, I beseeth you as strangers and pilgrims, abstain from fleshly lusts, which war against the soul.

John 10:10   The thief cometh not, but for to steal, and to kill, and to destroy.

The devil has a mission which is to steal, kill and destroy the three fold nature of man. So the antidote for demonic invasion is that man will abstain from fleshly lusts, which war against his soul. Satan launches out demonic attacks against the soul - nature of man, influencing him to experience personality changes that can cause him to be insane or psychotic, often experiencing suicidal tendencies.

Matthew 17:15 - 18   Lord have mercy on my son: for he is lunatic, and sore vexed: for ofttimes he falleth into the fire, and oft into the water. And I brought him to thy disciples, and they could not cure him. Then Jesus answered and said, O faithless and perverse generation, have long shall I be with you? How long shall I suffer you? Bring him hither to me. And Jesus rebuked the devil: and he departed out of him: and the child was cured from that very hour.

In chapter I, I stated that the devil has a systematic, seductive plan to destroy man and bring the man into captivity, by three female spirits. Each of these three spirits attacks a specific area of the man's three fold nature.

- Delilah (the she devil) steals the man's body, Id and his priestly anointing for service
- Jezebel (the witch) destroys the man's spirit, ego and prophetic anointing.
- Athaliah (the terminator) she kills the man's soulish realm, his superego and his kingship.

Superego under Attack
(Athaliah kills the superego of the man)

As I stated earlier, the superego is the third component of the personality, it is the part of the personality that has aspirations and values that it wants to strive for. It also contains prohibitions and restrictions, that help to regulate mans behavior. The superego in pediphiles, serial killers and mass murderers, obviously, doesn't restrict the deviant behavior of these men to the law's of society. The spirit of Athaliah can manifest herself through a male or female. Because she has no respect for men and desires to destroy them, it doesn't matter what gender the spirit uses.

In Genesis 4th chapter, Athaliah attacks the superego of Cain. Because she controlled his superego his hatred against his brother Abel a righteous man was not restricted.

Genesis 4:5, 8	But unto Cain and to his offering he had not respect. And Cain was very wroth, and his countenance fell. And Cain talked with Abel his brother: and it came to pass, when they were in the field, that Cain rose up against Abel his brother, and slew him.

In Exodus 1st chapter, the spirit of Athaliah is shown controlling the superego of Pharaoh. In the chapter, the king (or Pharaoh) of Egypt issued a decree to kill all the Hebrew baby boys. Here this female terrorist tried to destroy the male deliverer, trying to stop the righteous seed of God, Israel's deliver Moses. This spirit knows no boundaries when it comes to killing and destroying the lives of babies and male children.

Exodus 1:15 - 16	And the king of Egypt spake to the Hebrew midwives, of which the name of the one was Shiphrah, and the name of the other Puah: And he said when you do the office of a midwife to the Hebrew women, and see them upon the stools, if it be a son, then ye shall kill him: but if it be a daughter, then she shall live.

The spirit of Athaliah tried to annihilate or destroy the prophecy of the male deliverer Moses and indirectly to stop the male deliverer Jesus Christ our wonderful counselor, the everlasting father, and prince of peace that was coming through the Davidic line to reconcile man back to God.

>Genesis 3:15   And I will put enmity between thee and the woman, and between thy seed and her seed; it shall bruise thy head, and thou shalt bruise his heel.

Satan commission the spirit of Athaliah to kill the righteous male see of God, she wants to prevent man's reconciliation back to God and satan's defeat by the righteous seed of God, His son Jesus Christ. Finally, I note that this spirit comes up against the Christ child, the anointed seed of God. Athaliah controlled the superego of King Herod, and he sent out a decree to kill all children under the age of two years old, trying to stop the promise covenant of God.

>Matthew 2:16   Then Herod, when he saw that he was mocked of the wise men, was exceeding wroth, and sent forth, and slew all the children that were in Bethlehem, and in all the coasts thereof, from two years

old and under, according to the time which he had diligently inquired of the wise men.

The spirit of Athaliah kills the male's superego inhibiting him from making accomplishments. Because of the spirit of Athaliah she will leave a man with no aspiration for enhancing his life style. He never achieves any of his goals because the spirit of Athaliah keeps him in bondage in a defeated and apathetic lifestyle.

Athaliah kills His Kingship

Athaliah the queen-mother emasculated her son, from operating in his kingship. She was controlling and desired to be empowered. Today, we have many wives, mothers and sisters that have the spirit of Athaliah. They have emasculated the male-seed from reigning as king. Women with the spirit of Athaliah kill the male's superego by injecting her venom first through words.
Contrary to the popular rhyme sticks and stones may break my bones but words will never hurt us. The tongue has the power of life and death and words can destroy. Constantly telling the male, he'll never be a man, he's nothing, he's no good and other negative statements can destroy a man. Secondly women with the spirit of Athaliah can emasculate

males by extremely mothering him and making him a mama's boy, not allowing him to function as a man as she performs his role as king for him. Under the spirit's influence she never releases him to function in his God given destiny as an adult man or a king.

Therefore he will remain childish and irresponsible. The spirit of Athaliah will castrate his manhood and reduce him to childishness, never to reign in his kingship. This terminator's desire is to remove godly men from their place of authority and leadership. This demonic controlling spirit will even kill it's own offspring, attempting to do anything for empowerment.

Thirdly wives, girlfriends and women in general have lost their dignity as females, the weaker vessels. They have become more like men not only desiring his position but also his attire. There are many women that won't allow a man to be a gentleman, and the new society doesn't teach little boys to be gentleman and to respect the girls or women. There are women that will settle and not demand that their husband respect them or take accountability as the head of the family. The woman is forced to take over the office that God has ordained for men to occupy.

All of these are manifestations of Athaliah killing and destroying generations of men. Castrating them from what their Father created them to be when they are God's son, having his DNA, character and also his nature.

Examples of how some women can kill the male seed.

(1) Women that don't desire their man to work or pay bills. They desire to pay all the bills.
(2) Men that stay home and the woman works while he drives around in her car all day, while she provides the gas. When the bible says, "But if any provide not for his own, and especially for those of his own house, he has denied the faith, and is worst then an infidel. - (1 Timothy 5:8)"
(3) Men that is always looking to you for money, your food card and to buy his clothing.
(4) Women that are in agreement with men degrading the female in music, the Arts, conversation and in society.

These behaviors destroys a man and also what his true character is suppose to be. These are the reasons some men are not protective or respectful of women in general. At this point this type of man becomes a spirit son of Athaliah, becoming weak, worthless and ineffective.

Data relating to child homicide

Today, there are many women who are oppressed or possessed by the spirit of Athaliah, and they may experience an intense feeling of killing her seeds. As I was mediating the Lord began to give me divine insight. God allows me to visually see the spirit of Athaliah in operation today, with mothers and fathers that are actually killing their sons.

Here is some data that I pulled up in my research about the destructive nature of Athaliah's spirit.

- In 2001, North Fort Myers, Florida. A mother named Leslie Wallace, killed her six year old son James, then went to her son's Kenneth church. She shot at him but thank God, his bible saved him. She then went to her oldest son Gregory's work place to kill him but he had been warned.
  *Reference: ABC News.com (copyright @2010 - ABC News Internet Ventures)

- In October 1994. Susan Smith murder her two sons Michael and Alex as they slept strapped in their car seats and she drove her car into a lake before she got out of her car. At that time I questioned myself, how could a mother commit such an evil, diabolic crime against her children.
  *Reference: TruTv.com & Shotmug.com

- In May 2003, Deanna Laney was charged with murder in New Chapel Hill Texas for killing her two sons after calling 911 and stating "I've just killed my boys". March 29, 2004, she was charged with two counts of murder in the death

Three Occult Female Spirits

of Joshua 8 and Luke 6, also a single account to Aaron who survived.
  *Reference: Crime & Courts on MSNBC.com

- In June 2001, Andrea Yates of Houston Texas was charged with killing her five children, four of them were sons (Noah, John, Paul, & Luke). She then called the police and greeted him at her door, stating "I killed my children." She also called her husband at work to report what she had just done. Isn't it ironic, how these children names are basically biblical?
  *Reference: Karisable.com - 01/29/09

- In 2002, Dr. Ellen Feinberg in Bergen County, N.J. was charged with killing her son Adam and critically wounding her younger son Matthew.
  *Reference: Ssristories.com

- Caro Socorro was 42 when she killed her three sons, ages 5, 8 and 11, while Susan Eubanks was 33 when she killed her four sons, ages 4, 6, 7 and 14 in 1999.
  *Reference: Livesecure.org (2009)

- August 18, 2010, in Orangeburg S.C., Shaquan Duley killed her young sons, then strapped their lifeless bodies in their car seats while

rolling the vehicle in a South Carolina river in a desperate attempt to cover it up.
*Reference: Blackamericaweb.com

- October 01, 2001, A new Jersey father fatally shot his two teenage sons, critically wounded one more and set his home ablaze before police killed him, authorities said.
*Reference: Jason Kessler - CNN

- December 01, 2010, John Skelton, the father of missing Andrew Alexander and Tanner Skelton told the Morenci police that he has killed his sons.
*Reference: Examiner.com

Ephesians 6:12	For we wrestle not against flesh and blood, but against principalities, against powers, against the rulers of darkness of this world, against spiritual wickedness in high places.

This is the spirit of Athaliah, a ruling female terrorist. Satan has commissioned her to kill the male seed. He that has spiritual insight, let him see within the spirit realm. He that has ears, let him hear what the spirit of the Lord has said.

Ephesians 3:3 - 4	How that by revelation he made known unto me the mystery: (as I wrote afore in

few words, Whereby, when ye read, ye may understand my knowledge in the mystery of Christ).